LEMON
HEALTH BENEFITS

Lemons for Healthy Skin, Hair, Cleaning, and Weight Loss

Chris Shaw

Disclaimers

The author and publisher make no representation or warranties with respect to the accuracy, applicability, fitness, or completeness of the contents of this Ebook. The information contained in this Ebook is strictly for educational purposes. Therefore, if you wish to apply ideas contained in this Ebook, you are taking full responsibility for your actions.

The author and publisher disclaim any warranties (express or implied), merchantability, or fitness for any particular purpose. The author and publisher shall in no event be held liable to any party for any direct, indirect, punitive, special, incidental or other consequential damages arising directly or indirectly from any use of this material, which is provided "as is", and without warranties.

As always, the advice of a competent legal, tax, accounting or other professional should be sought. The author and publisher do not warrant the performance, effectiveness or applicability of any sites listed or linked to in this Ebook. All links are for information purposes only and are not warranted for content, accuracy or any other implied or explicit purpose.

Medical Disclaimer

The information provided in this should not be construed as personal medical advice or instruction. No action should be taken based solely on the contents of this site.

Readers should consult appropriate health professionals on any matter relating to their health and well-being.

The information and opinions provided here are believed to be accurate and sound, based on the best judgment available to the authors, but readers who fail to consult appropriate health authorities assume the risk of any injuries. This website is not responsible for errors or omissions.

Table of Contents

Health Benefits of Lemons: Introduction

Lemons offer far more than delicious smells and a sour flavor. This small, bright yellow fruit comes with many potential uses, from cleaning your home to improving your health. Add flavor to delicious dishes, treat skin problems, improve your hair, or add years to your life by harnessing the power of the lemon.

The power of lemons has been used for centuries. Lemons have been a popular cooking ingredient and cure-all in Asian countries, especially since the lemon tree is native to the area. Although lemon trees are native to Asia, eventually lemon trees were cultivated in Europe, and later, Christopher Columbus would introduce them to the Americas.

Although multiple types of lemons exist, different types of lemons generally contain about the same amounts of nutrients.

One raw lemon without its peel has only 17 calories, 0.6 grams of protein, and 0.2 grams of fat. Unlike many other fruits, lemons are very low in sugar with only 1.5 grams of sugar per lemon. Of course, lemons are well known for their high vitamin C content, and a single lemon offers you approximately 51% of your daily vitamin C needs. Other important vitamins and minerals found in lemons include:

Phosphorus
 Vitamin B6
 Thiamin
 Copper
 Iron
 Riboflavin
 Manganese
 Potassium
 Magnesium
 Calcium
 Pantothenic acid

Since lemons are packed with so many important vitamins and minerals, they offer some excellent health benefits. According to Medical News Today, some of the potential health benefits of consuming lemons regularly include maintaining healthy skin, cancer prevention, a stronger immune system, decreased risk of heart disease, and a lower risk of obesity.

Of course, while adding lemons to your food or drinks offer many health benefits, lemons also offer some incredible beauty benefits as well. Eating lemons is known for improving skin health, but lemons can be used topically for beautiful skin as well. From exfoliating your skin to healing breakouts, lemons provide an excellent, all-natural skincare treatment. Lemons can also be used on your hair for shiny, healthy hair.

Beyond the beauty benefits of lemons, lemons can also be used for eco-friendly, safe cleaning in your home. Instead of using cleaners that are packed with toxic chemicals, lemons can be used for cleaning the bathroom, your kitchen, and more. Not only are they an eco-friendly choice, but cleaning with lemons leaves your home smelling wonderful when you're done.

Cooking with lemon is a great way to enjoy the health benefits of lemons while adding flavor to your favorite dishes. Lemons amp up the flavor of chicken, add a zing to your favorite soups, and turn desserts into something special.

If you're not using the small but powerful lemon regularly, you're missing all the incredible benefits lemons have to offer. If you're ready to start reaping the benefits of lemons, here's a closer look at the health benefits of lemons, drinking warm lemon water, how to use lemons for beauty purposes, information on cleaning with lemons, and so much more.

Overall Health Benefits of Lemons

You don't really consider lemons to be one of the foods that are a powerhouse when it comes to nutrition. In fact, the simple little lemon has a lot to offer when it comes to overall good health and great nutrition.

Lemons are slightly oval and depending on the variety, they feature very thin smooth skin or a thicker dappled and textured skin. Again, depending on the variety that you get, they are sweet or quite sour. The very acidic taste comes from citric acid that is a part and parcel of what's good for you in the lemon.

Originally lemons were grown as a hybrid cross between a citron and a lime. They are believed to have originated in East and have been known to be cultivated for consumption for more than 2500 years. They were brought to Europe by Arabic travelers in about the 1100s. The Crusaders are given credit with bringing them back to England and other parts of Europe when they traveled in and around Palestine.

Like many other citrus fruits, lemons are packed with flavonoids. These compounds feature anti cancer properties as well as antioxidant properties. ***Some lemons can actually prevent the division of cells that cause cancer***. In addition to these awesome benefits, both lemons and limes are an outstanding source of Vitamin C. Vitamin C is an antioxidant and one of the most important ones that we find in nature.

What Vitamin C does is to travel throughout our bodies and neutralize the free radicals that it contacts in the fluid areas of the body. It neutralizes those both inside and outside the cell.

Free radicals can cause problems inside the body by damaging membranes, causing inflammatory responses and are known to be responsible for some autoimmune responses.

Because free radicals may be a causative agent in autoimmune disorders, Vitamin C has been reviewed and is considered one type of treatment for lowering the inflammation that can occur with diseases such as Rheumatoid and osteo arthritis.

Free radicals may also damage the vessels of the body and can allow cholesterol to build up in the system. Vitamin C is a helpful preventive measure for heart disease and is known for slowing the progression of atherosclerosis.

All in all, Vitamin C has some surprising benefits. Just a small amount of this water soluble vitamin can be remarkably helpful to your body. Vitamin C and specifically that which is found in lemons and limes has been shown to reduce the risk of mortality from nearly every causative factor, including cancer, stroke, and heart disease.

One quarter cup of lemon juice offers 31 percent of the Recommended daily value of Vitamin C and about 3 percent of the recommended daily value of Folate.

Drinking with Warm Lemon Water - You'll Be Amazed

A nice, warm drinking of a glass of water with lemon in the morning helps get your body going when you get out of bed. If you're starting your morning with a hot cup of tea or coffee, you may want to change your morning beverage to a nice mg of warm lemon water.

When you have a glass of water, you probably drink it cold. However, Ayurvedic medicine teaches that drinking warm water, particularly in the morning, has the power to heal your body. Adding lemons to that warm water offers even more great benefits. Lemons are known for their immune boosting, antiviral, and antibacterial powers, not to mention, they're packed with important nutrients.

The Benefits of Drinking Warm Lemon Water

Why should you begin drinking warm lemon water each morning? If you're not convinced that you should give up your coffee for a mug of warm lemon water, here's a look at the benefits you can enjoy when you make warm lemon water part of your daily routine.

Benefit #1 – Improves Digestion

The combination of lemon juice and warm water improves digestion. The lemon water also helps to stimulate your digestive system, encouraging the liver to product bile, which is needed for digestion. You may also notice that you have fewer problems with bloating, gas, and heartburn when you drink warm lemon water daily. Most people notice that they no longer have problems with constipation as well.

Benefit #2 – Gives Your Immune System a Boost

The high amount of vitamin C in the lemon juice helps to give your immune system a boost. Saponins, found in lemons, have antimicrobial properties that may help prevent colds and the flu.

Benefit #3 – Flushes Away Toxins

Lemon juice is a mild diuretic, and the combination of lemon juice and warm water helps the body flush away toxins and waste. The citric acid found in lemons helps to maximize enzyme function in the body, stimulating the liver and aiding in detoxification. Increasing your water intake by drinking warm lemon water also helps to body flush away toxins more efficiently.

Benefit #4 – Aids in Weight Loss

If you want to shed a few pounds, warm lemon water can help. Drinking warm lemon water helps to increase your metabolic rate. It also helps to break down body fat. The pectin fiber in the lemons help to decrease food cravings, making it easier for you to avoid cravings throughout your day.

Benefit #5 – Reduces Inflammation

One of the main causes of inflammation in the body is uric acid. Uric acid often builds up in joints, resulting in inflammation and pain. Lemon water helps to remove uric acid, reducing inflammation through the body. By reducing inflammation, you may notice that you deal with less pain as well.

Benefit #6 – Improves Skin

Drinking water has the power to clear skin and the addition of the vitamin C from the lemons helps to improve skin too. Vitamin C helps to reduce problems with blemishes while combatting free radicals that can cause skin damage and aging. Start drinking warm lemon water each morning and you'll notice a big change in your skin over time.

Benefit #7 – Balances Your Body's pH

While lemons taste acidic, when the lemon water enters your body, it has an alkalizing effect. For optimal health, your body should be more alkaline, and drinking warm lemon water daily helps to balance your body's pH so it's more alkaline. This makes it easier for your body to resist sickness and disease.

How to Make Your Warm Lemon Water

Now that you're aware of all the benefits of drinking warm lemon water, you may be wondering how you should make this healthy drink. You need to start with purified water and fresh, organic lemons. You should never use bottled lemon juice to make your lemon water. Make sure that your water is warm, but it shouldn't be scalding hot. Squeeze about ½ of a lemon into a mug or glass of 8-12 ounces of warm water. You can also add a bit of honey to the water if desired for a hint of sweetness and additional health benefits.

When to Drink the Warm Lemon Water

When should you drink the warm lemon water? The best time to drink this warm beverage is first thing in the morning. When you first get up, drink the water before you eat or drink anything else. After drinking your water, make sure you give it 30-60 minutes before you eat anything so it has a chance to go through your digestive system before you begin adding food to your stomach. Of course, you can also have a mug of the warm lemon water in the evening as well.

NOTE: The acids in lemons can be hard on your teeth. Avoid brushing your teeth right after drinking the lemon water.

Healthier, Prettier Skin from Lemons

Beauty is a lot more than skin deep. Did you know that some of the cosmetics that you use every day may contain toxins that can disrupt hormones and cause cancer?

No matter what your age you want your skin to look as good as it can look but you also want to keep it healthy. Lemons can help you to keep your skin looking good. Supple, smooth skin is something that you can get naturally without the many costly and often toxic skin care products such as bleaches, lighteners, lotions and hair rinses.

Lemon juice is something that is easy to find, cost effective and can take the place of other more costly beauty and skin care products.

Lemons are natural cleansers, have astringent properties and can lighten the skin naturally. Curious about what else they can do for you?

How to Use Lemon Juice on Your Skin

Lemon juice can be an active part of any moisturizer. One of the best is to mix lemon and honey in equal parts and pat it onto your skin in the dry areas. If you have exceedingly dry skin, add a tablespoon of olive oil. Your very dry skin will benefit from the natural oils and from the lemon.

Do you need a good exfoliator that is natural? Lemon removes dead cells naturally.

Here's How To Do It:

Cut your lemon into four parts, exposing the inner flesh of the lemon. Dip it into brown sugar and scrub it gently across your face to remove the dead skin cells. Rinse well when you've finished removing any trace of the lemon and sugar.

Use lemon juice to clear away blackheads. Not only can you lower the appearance of blackheads but you may also be able to prevent their occurrence. Rub lemon juice on them every night until they are gone. Make sure that you wash off the lemon juice in the morning and in between times, use a gentle soap and keep your skin very clean.

Lemon Juice may also help you to lower the incidence of skin wrinkles. Mix a little lemon with some honey and olive oil to create a lotion. Use the lotion on your face for about 10-20 minutes. Don't use it in the eyes, but you may add it to the area around the eye. It won't happen instantly but over time the wrinkles will begin to go away. Use this mixture only about every other day.

Lemon juice can also help to lighten your skin slightly and to fade skin spots and even freckles? It may take about two weeks to work, but use fresh lemon juice on the skin at night before you retire. In the morning be sure that you wash your face well with mild soap to remove the lemon juice. Bear in mind that if you are using this method, it may be drying to your skin. If you begin to see some dry spots, apply a moisturizer—even one with lemon. Plain lemon juice on the skin every day can cause some dryness particularly if left on the skin for a longer period of time.

Lemon juice and lemons may offer you the means to moisturize, to cleanse to lighten skin and to provide you with a great toner and astringent, all without adding anything toxic or unhealthy to your skin.

Lemons for Irresistible Hair

Lemons are a great haircare ingredient. Lemons have powerful properties that can help you achieve the beautiful, healthy hair that you desire.

Lemons contain plenty of vitamin C, which means they're great for brightening hair. Since they have anti-inflammatory properties, they are great for treating scalp problems. The juice from a lemon can even help you control dandruff. Here's a look at some of the best ways you can use lemons for gorgeous hair.

Lemon Dandruff Treatment

If you're dealing with dandruff, lemons can eliminate the problem. Mix some fresh lemon juice with some warm olive oil. Rub the mixture onto your scalp and leave for 30 minutes. Rinse away the mixture and shampoo as normal. The lemon juice helps to remove dandruff and the olive oil moisturizes the scalp. You may notice a bit of tingling on the scalp from the lemon juice. Don't use this treatment more than once weekly.

Lemon Hair Loss Treatment

If you are dealing with hair loss, the vitamins in lemon juice may help. Combine the juice of one lemon with an equal amount of coconut water. Massage the mixture into your scalp and leave on your hair for 30-60 minutes. Do this once weekly to reinvigorate the scalp and stimulate hair growth.

Naturally Bleach Hair with Lemon

If you want to lighten your hair or add some natural looking highlights, consider using lemons. Lemons offer an all-natural, chemical free way to lighten your hair. Put some lemon juice in a spray bottle and spray on hair. If you just want highlights, apply to only certain areas of your hair. Sit outside and let your hair dry in the sun. You may need to repeat this process several times to see significant results. This usually works best on people with lighter hair.

Anti-Buildup Lemon Treatment

Over time, shampoo and styling products can build up in your hair. That buildup can leave your hair limp and heavy. You can use a lemon treatment to remove buildup and excess oil. To remove buildup, gently massage a couple tablespoons of lemon juice through your hair. Rinse the lemon juice away after a couple minutes. It should eliminate buildup without removing the natural oils that your hair needs.

Lemon Leave-In Conditioner

A leave-in conditioner often makes it easier for you to detangle hair after you wash it. It also keeps ends moisturized, even if you use heat treatments on your hair. Instead of paying big bucks for a leave-in conditioner packed with chemicals, make your own lemon based leave in conditioner. You'll need one cup of water, 1 pack of plain gelatin, 4 tablespoons of fresh aloe vera, 2 teaspoons of coconut oil, and 2 tablespoons of freshly squeezed lemon juice. To make the conditioner, mix the gelatin and water together in a saucepan over medium heat until the gelatin has dissolved. After the gelatin dissolves, add the lemon juice. Allow to cool until you have a gel. Place the gel, coconut oil, and the aloe vera into a blender or food processor. Blend until you have a smooth, creamy mixture. Use the same way you would any other leave-in conditioner.

Why and How to Clean with Lemons

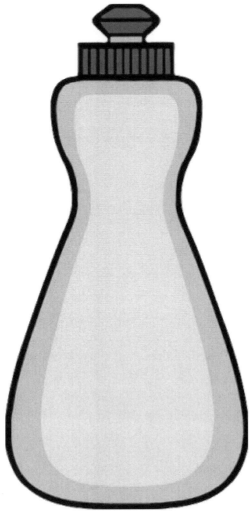

Lemons are good for more than just fighting disease. They can help you to fight the damage that comes to home and family from high residue cleaners. In many cases, the cleaners that we are using are damaging to our good health.

Why Clean With Lemons?

Chemicals in household cleaners, even including the fragrances may be toxic. Because the formulas of these cleaners are protected, they are not required to list the ingredients, but may state simply, fragrance. OSHA found that more than a third of the chemicals used in the fragrance of household cleaners are toxins. According to Organic Consumer.org, "sudsing agents [such as] diethanolamine (DEA) and triethanolamine (TEA). When these substances come into contact with nitrites, often present as undisclosed preservatives or contaminants, they react to form nitrosamines - carcinogens that readily penetrate the skin."

That's what makes the small but mighty lemon such a good bet. Natural disinfectants, lemons can offer you a sparkling clean and a healthier home. The acidic content of the lemon means that you can disinfect your home naturally while leaving it sparkling clean.

Use Lemons and Lemon Juice for:

Cleaning your cutting board.

Rub the lemon on the stains that exist on the cutting board and allow it to remain until the stains begin to fade. The lemon also disinfects the surface of the cutting board at the same time it is removing the stains.

Want cleaner countertops?

For a laminate counter, gently roll the lemon to break the inner pieces and then cut your lemon in half cross wise. Squeeze out a reasonable amount of juice from the lemon. Work the juice over the stains on the counter and using the lemon itself as a means to scrub the counter, rub stained areas or dirty areas gently. If you're not able to procure fresh lemons a bottle of concentrated lemon juice will do the job just as well.

Want to clean those white clothes without using chemicals such as chlorine?

Your lemon will do the job very nicely. Simply mix a 3/4 cup of lemon juice into a gallon of water that is very hot. Immerse the clothing and allow it to soak. This is a great cure-all for stained cotton and other natural clothing but may not work well for silk or other finer cloth. The clothing can soak for up to an hour or more. If it requires an overnight stay in the solution, it's still perfectly safe so long as you're not using fine materials such as silken clothing. Take the clothing out of the solution and put them into the washer. Use the remaining solution to dump into the washer with your clothing. You can't over-bleach your clothes using lemon juice and it's safe to be combined with most mild clothes washing detergent.

Cleaning copper plates with lemon juice

Cut the lemon in half (again, cross wise) and sprinkle salt onto the lemon. Using it as a scrubber, clean the bottoms of copper pans and other copper items. The lemon juice will nicely remove the tarnish that has appeared on your copper over time.

Protecting your home and family is part of what you do. Use natural lemon and other natural methods of cleaning for cleaner, safer home care that leaves no residue.

Cosmetic Uses with Lemons

The versatility of lemons makes them great for cooking, flavoring your drinks, encouraging healthy hair, and more. You can also start adding lemons to your beauty routine, since they have so many cosmetic benefits. Instead of paying big bucks for cosmetic products and treatments, try using these lemon juice cosmetic treatments.

Nail Strengthener

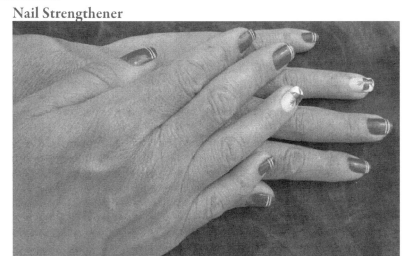

If you want beautiful, healthy nails, lemon juice is a wonderful nail strengthener. To strengthen nails, make a solution of lemon juice and olive oil. Soak fingernails in the solution for ten minutes. Rinse away the lemon and oil with some warm water. Not only will you notice that nails are stronger, but the lemon juice helps to soften cuticles and remove any leftover dark or yellowish tinge that has been left behind by dark nail polish.

Eliminate Dark Skin on Elbows and Knees

If your elbows or knees are dark and dry, lemon juice can help soften the skin and eliminate the darkness. Make a paste out of baking soda and lemon juice. Scrub the paste into knees and elbows to help remove tough, dead skin. Rinse with a bit of lemon juice and water. The lemon juice will also help to bleach the dark skin so your elbows and knees do not look as dark. Make sure you moisturize well after using the lemon treatment.

Eliminate Excess Oil

Are you tired of having a shiny forehead and chin throughout the day? Before you apply your makeup, apply a <u>lemon based skin toner</u>. Make your own skin toner by combining a tablespoon of witch hazel, two tablespoons of vodka, two tablespoons of lemon juice, and one tablespoon of distilled water. Mix well in a bottle. Apply with a cotton ball to skin to eliminate oil before applying your makeup. You will notice that this toner helps to fight oil all day long.

Deal with a Streaky Home Tan

There's nothing worse than dealing with a streaky orange tan. If you do not want to look like a pumpkin, grab a lemon to deal with the problem. Cut the lemon in half and rub the cut end over the area that has streaked. Continue rubbing over the area until the tan looks even and natural. Allow skin to dry and then gently wash away the lemon juice. Since lemon juice makes skin more sensitive to the sun, keep skin well protected from the sun for the next few days.

Exfoliate Lips

If your lips have dead skin on them, you will not get the smooth, beautiful look you want when applying your lipstick. To exfoliate your lips, combine some fresh lemon juice with a drop of glycerin. Apply to lips and leave on overnight. The lemon helps exfoliate skin and the glycerin moisturizes your lips. If you have dark lips, this combination can help lighten lips as well. After exfoliating and moisturizing with your lemon and glycerin mixture, lips will be smooth the next day. You'll have a perfect base for your lipstick.

Understanding Lemon Essential Oil

Lemon, also known as Citrus Limon, is a natural fruit containing—as most fruits do—an essential oil. One of the most important things to know about lemon essential oil is that it contains limonene.

<u>Lemon essential oil</u> is the oil that is expressed from the lemon, primarily the peels supply the essential oils although it is found throughout the fruit. It is one of the most versatile of the essential oils. It is also highly sustainable. When is the last time you heard of a lemon shortage?

The lemon oil is expressed in multiple ways. Dependent upon the methodology used, the properties of the lemon essential oil will also change. One example of this is in the degree of phototoxicity.

Lemon essential oils that are distilled by steam are not considered to be phototoxic oil. When lemon essential oil is cold pressed from the lemon, it is considered to be phototoxic. That is to say that it will cause damage when exposed to ultraviolet light. There are natural chemicals present in certain essential oils that can cause reddening, blistering and burning of the skin when UV light rays hit the oils. As a general rule, citrus fruits contain the furanocoumarins that are thought to cause the phototoxicity.

It is for this reason that if you have used lemon essential oil to create a skin cream or to treat freckles, lighten your skin and for other reasons, you'll usually read that you should use it at night and wash it off in the morning.

It requires more than 1500 lemons to make one pound of the essential lemon oil. It's also one of the best ways to clean, to treat your skin, and is outstanding for aroma therapy. Lemon oil when diffused into a room can remove smoke smells such as from cigarette smoke or even from a kitchen incident. It's also said to help to bring clearer thought processes as well as to lift the mood of those who are affected by seasonal mood swings.

The reality is that lemon oil is good for just about anything and everything. Some of the uses for lemon essential oil include:

- Diffusion to lift the mood or remove odors from the household. Use Lemon oil in a diffuser in place of the unnatural and chemical sprays that are used in many households.
- Lemon essential oil also purifies the air.
- It can be used to kill specific types of mold and to prevent its regrowth.
- Lemon essential oil can remove warts, treat corns and callouses and help to smooth your skin.

If you're using lemon essential oil for your skin or body during the daytime, stay out of the sunlight for about 8 hours.

The Basics of Cooking with Lemons

Used in a variety of forms, a hint of lemon can breathe new life into even the most dull or bland tasting dish. In fact, with the exception of the various types of salt and pepper, cooks probably use lemon more than any other flavoring. Lemons lend a lively flavor and a crisp aroma to nearly everything from meat, marinades, and vegetables to baked goods and sauces. Like any good ingredient, lemon serves not only to lend its own unique flavor, but to enhance the other flavors of the dish as well.

The varieties of lemon most commonly found in grocery stores are the Eureka and the Lisbon. The Lisbon is slightly smaller than the Eureka and is usually available even during the winter months. Where flavor is concerned, there is very little difference between them and most shoppers can't even tell them apart. When choosing a lemon, look for one that feels heavy, gives slightly when squeezed, and doesn't have a thick feeling rind. Since lemons change from green to yellow due to changes in temperature rather than ripeness, some green patches won't affect the taste; brown spots however, indicate rot.

Aside from using lemon slices or wedges as a garnish for your dish (usually seafood), the most frequently called for parts of the lemon are the juice and the zest; many recipes call for both. Juice and zest are both wonderful additions, but when added to a dish they each contribute a slightly different characteristic.

Lemon Juice

An average sized lemon holds just around ¼ cup of juice. To maximize the amount of juice and make it easier to squeeze, allow lemons to come to room temperature or microwave it for 15 to 20 seconds. Before juicing the lemon, apply a slight amount of pressure and roll it around the counter with your hand. This will rupture the juice filled cells that make up the lemon and make extracting the juice much easier. Lemon juice adds a tangy aspect to your dish as well as brightening the flavors.

Lemon Zest

The zest of a lemon is the outermost, shiny yellow part of the skin. The zest contains the essential oils of the lemon, which are the most powerful compounds in terms of flavor. The white part of the peel that lies just under the zest should not be used because it is very bitter. When zesting, remove just the dark yellow part of the peel. The zest will add the bright flavor and aroma of lemon without the tartness associated with lemon juice.

Lemons and Food

The acidic nature of lemons causes them to react differently with different foods. For example, lemons are commonly used in marinades for fish or seafood. The acid will actually denature the proteins found in these foods and as a result, the flesh comes opaque and firm, much as if it is already cooked.

Lemon juice, as well as other acidic liquids, is commonly thought to tenderize red meat while it marinates; this isn't strictly true. While marinating, the acid does help to disjoin the bonds between the proteins and causes them to loosen up, after a period of time they tighten again. Not only does the meat remain tough, in tightening up, the natural juices are squeezed out of the meat and it becomes very dry when cooked. Another reason that marinades don't truly tenderize meat is that they rarely penetrate deeply enough to make a real difference. Using an injector helps to a certain extent, but unless you have a very thin cut of meat, marinate won't make a significant difference in the tenderness.

No matter what you are marinating, one of the most important things to remember is not to over-marinate it because it. This is particularly important with seafood, which can become very rubbery.

Lemon can be used to liven up any type of cuisine and the only mistake that can be made is to use too much. The next time you have a dish that just seems to be missing something, try a splash of fresh lemon juice. Even if you use an amount so small that it can't be tasted, you'll be amazed at how it will liven up the other flavors of the dish. Don't constrain lemons to seafood, try a squeeze on chicken, pork, and even pasta and you will be astounded by the results.

50 Lemon Recipes

Breakfast:

Lemon Rolls
http://www.lovefromtheoven.com/2015/03/19/lemon-rolls/
Category: Breakfast
These are like cinnamon rolls, but for lemons and they are tasty! Find out the secret ingredient used to make this have an extra yummy punch.

Grandma's Lemon Bars
http://alidaskitchen.com/2012/10/04/grandmas-lemon-bars-12-weeks-of-christmas-treats/
Category: Breakfast
Who doesn't love grandma and her lemon bars? These are just plain yummy!

Bakery Style Blueberry-Lemon Muffins
http://thecafesucrefarine.com/2014/04/bakery-style-blueberry-lemon-muffins/
Category: Breakfast
Blueberry muffins are usually pretty delicious, but blueberry-lemon muffins are fantastic. And the layer of crumb-topping makes it complete.

Lemon Ricotta Pancakes
http://www.cookingclassy.com/2014/02/lemon-ricotta-pancakes/
Category: Breakfast
Pancakes are a must in most homes. Here is a new twist to pancakes. And yes, you'll find cheese in this recipe. Try it, you'll like it.

Lemon Chia Seed Protein Cookies

http://amyshealthybaking.com/blog/2015/02/28/lemon-chia-seed-protein-cookies/

Category: Breakfast

Packed with protein and healthy goodness, these are a perfect for an on the go treat or even breakfast.

Lemon & Quinoa Breakfast Bowl

https://www.youtube.com/watch?v=_uW7xqjKRaw

Category: Breakfast

Fun, tasty & mostly healthy. This is great to get you energized in the morning.

Blueberry Lemon Breakfast Cake

https://www.youtube.com/watch?v=UOQU_-lYro0

Category: Breakfast

Are you planning a brunch get together? This paired with a fun drink would be perfect for that!

Lemon Apple Juice

https://youtu.be/cKUZFaIlts8

Category: Breakfast

This is the perfect wake you up and helps keep your body healthy. Try this tasty dish!

Lemon Poppyseed Scones

https://www.youtube.com/watch?v=ZlBtospiMOA

Category: Breakfast

This is easy, tasty and makes the house smell delicious! And it takes under 10 minutes to get create.

Lunch:

Lemon Chicken Orzo Soup
http://damndelicious.net/2014/04/25/lemon-chicken-orzo-soup/
Category: Lunch
Looking for something light and easy? You'll love this soup.
Add a pinch of pepper and you'll come back for more
Lemon Rosemary Pork Chops With Arugula Salad
http://www.healthyseasonalrecipes.com/lemon-rosemary-pork-chops-with-arugula-salad/
Category: Lunch
Sometimes lunch or dinner calls for grilling out and this dish is ready! Best of all? It doesn't require you to marinade it for hours. You can just make it, grill it and then enjoy it.
Tomato, Onion & Roasted Lemon Salad
http://theviewfromgreatisland.com/2014/08/minimal-monday-tomato-onion-roasted-lemon-salad.html
Category: Lunch
This is a colorful treat! You get so many great nutrients and its easy to make and something new to try.
Easy Lemon Chicken
http://damndelicious.net/2014/01/22/easy-lemon-chicken/
Category: Lunch
A 5 ingredient meal that's tasty and easy? You're welcome! This will have your mouth watering and your mind blown with how easy and yummy Easy Lemon Chicken is.
Rosemary Lemon Turkey Burger
http://www.thekitchenprepblog.com/2014/06/gourmet-summer-grilling-with.html

Category: Lunch

This is not your typical backyard burger, it is better! It's packed with flavor and fun.

Quinoa, Asparagus, Pea & Lemon Salad
http://www.tamingtwins.com/2014/05/27/quinoa-asparagus-pea-and-lemon-salad/

Category: Lunch

This won't make you want to take a nap, promise! This will give you that mid afternoon boost you need to get productive.

Dinner:

Honey Lemon Chicken With Angel Hair Pasta
http://www.averiecooks.com/2015/04/honey-lemon-chicken-with-angel-hair-pasta.html
Category: Dinner
When you put lemon, pasta and chicken together, you create heaven. This recipe is a tasty treat and easy to make. It's so colorful and perfect for any season.

Lemon Butter Chicken
http://damndelicious.net/2014/12/31/lemon-butter-chicken/
Category: Dinner
This recipe is protein rich and is a family favorite. The creamy butter sauce that covers the chicken is a decadent delight.

Lemon Garlic Herb Crusted Salmon
http://www.mynaturalfamily.com/recipes/clean-eating-recipes/easy-baked-fish-recipe/
Category: Dinner
If you need a fast meal to make, prep & cook time total 25 minutes for this tasty fish dish. This recipe can also be used with most fish types and come out deliciously.

Charred Lemon Chicken Piccata
http://www.myrecipes.com/m/recipe/charred-lemon-chicken-piccata
Category: Dinner
Did you know lightly charring the lemons makes them taste better? Neither did we! Try this and you will surely fall in love.

Asian Lemon Chicken
http://www.eazypeazymealz.com/asian-lemon-chicken/
Category: Dinner
This is a favorite at most Asian restaurants but it can get pretty pricey. Here is less expensive, more delicious way to make this classic at home.

Lemon Chicken With Asparagus & Potatoes
http://damndelicious.net/2015/03/20/lemon-chicken-with-asparagus-and-potatoes/
Category: Dinner
This is a great recipe and a full meal in just one dish. Plus, its tasty and perfect for any dinner party that you host.

Creamy Lemon Chicken Pasta
http://www.scatteredthoughtsofacraftymom.com/2012/08/creamy-lemon-chicken-pasta.html?m=1
Category: Dinner
Are weeknights hectic? This is the perfect solution for a quick and easy, yet still scrumptious meal. Plus, it is still delicious for tomorrow's reheated lunch.

Lemon Chicken Fettuccine
http://diethood.com/lemon-chicken-fettuccine/
Category: Dinner
If you love chicken & pasta, this is screaming your name. This fettuccine is bright and colorful and fills you up!

Garlic Lemon Pork
http://www.marthastewart.com/925230/garlic-lemon-pork
Category: Dinner
This is a delicious meal and best of all, you could trade out the pork for chicken or turkey breasts and it will still be equally as delicious.

Slow Cooker Lemon Chicken
http://www.number-2-pencil.com/2013/05/23/slow-cooker-lemon-garlic-chicken/
Category: Dinner
Just throw it in the slow cooker and it is good to go.. If you know you are going to have a busy day, pop this in before work and voila! It's ready when you get home.

Greek Lemon Chicken & Potatoes
https://www.youtube.com/watch?v=h6OSMbfhIao
Category: Dinner

Here is a yummy and funny video on how to create Greek Lemon Chicken. You also get tasty potatoes too!

Desserts:

The Best Lemon Loaf (Better Than Starbucks Copycat)
http://www.averiecooks.com/2015/01/best-lemon-loaf-better-starbucks-copycat.html
Category: Dessert
This is a yummy copycat. Could it really be better than Starbucks? You betcha! Come taste

Lemon Crinkle Cookies
http://lovetobeinthekitchen.com/2012/09/06/lemon-crinkle-cookies/
Category: Desserts
If you have kids, these are easy and fun to get the kids involved. If no little ones, these are easy for you too!

Lemon-Strawberry Petit Fours
http://thedomesticrebel.com/2012/04/14/lemon-strawberry-petit-fours/
Category: Desserts
These just look so fun and tasty. Cake-like plus sprinkles? Need I say more?

Lemon Meringue Pie
https://www.youtube.com/watch?v=gd-Ruxza-8A
Category: Dessert
This is a holiday favorite and tastes so yummy! Watch the great video to learn how to make your own tasty pie.

No Bake Golden Oreo Lemon Dessert
http://www.crazyforcrust.com/2014/03/bake-golden-oreo-lemon-dessert/
Category: Dessert
Do we even need to talk about how yummy this is? Anything with oreos means we're winning.

Lemon Panna Cotta with Driscoll's Berry Compote

http://www.momontimeout.com/2013/06/lemon-panna-cotta-with-driscolls-berries-compote/
Category: Dessert
This is a fun and airy, you'll love this sweet treat! And it looks really pretty too!
No Bake Lemon Cheesecake Mousse Cups
http://overtimecook.com/2013/05/12/no-bake-lemon-cheesecake-mousse-cups/
Category: Dessert
No baking & Cheesecake? Yes please! These bite sized treats are great for parties!
Lemon Pull Apart Bread
http://www.barbarabakes.com/lemon-pull-apart-bread-a-giveaway/
Category: Dessert
This will melt in your mouth and make you feel like you're eating a piece of heaven. The icing on top is just as tasty as the bread itself.
Triple Lemon Cake
http://www.lifeloveandsugar.com/2012/08/31/triple-lemon-cake/
Category: Dessert
When you're a cake lover, you don't need a reason to eat cake. We wanted to share just one reason for you to eat this cake: It's delicious.
Lemon Truffles
http://letthebakingbeginblog.com/2013/12/when-life-gives-you-lemonsmake-lemon-truffles/
Category: Desserts
These will have you drooling as you make them and enjoy the yummy chocolate middle!
Sugar Cookie Lemon Tarts
http://inquiringchef.com/2013/08/20/sugar-cookie-lemon-tarts/

Category: Desserts

These are small yummy treats, but they sure do pack a punch. They are easy to make and delicious!

Easy Lemon Brownies

https://www.youtube.com/watch?v=b0k5wqAu1aM

Category: Desserts

This is super easy to create and you'll have your yummy brownies in the oven within 8 minutes!

Glazed Lemon Blueberry Scones

http://blog.thelovenerds.com/2014/04/glazed-lemon-blueberry-scones.html

Category: Desserts

These scones are unlike any other scones. How? Make them and you'll see.

Beverages:

Lemon Cream Soda
http://jensfavoritecookies.com/2013/08/09/lemon-cream-sodas-and-a-big-announcement/
Category: Beverages
This is a fun and refreshing drink. It's easy to make and fun for the whole family to enjoy.

Copycat Sonic's Lemonberry Slush
http://jennifersikora.com/2013/06/copycat-recipe-sonics-lemonberry-slush/
Category: Beverage
Need a refreshing drink? This is it! Yummy, easy and almost just as tasty as Sonic's.

Blueberry Lemonade
http://damndelicious.net/2014/05/07/blueberry-lemonade/
Category: Beverage
This is wonderfully juicy and when you add blueberries even into your drink, you're in for a fun treat!

Adult Beverages:

Lemon Drop Martini
http://asouthernfairytale.com/2014/08/07/lemon-drop-martini-recipe/
Category: Adult Beverages
You've had a long week and you just need some revitalizing, delicious and filled with alcohol. You're covered. This is a tangy and fun treat for you to relax with.

Lemon Meringue Martini
http://www.lemontreedwelling.com/2013/04/lemon-meringue-martini.html
Category: Adult Beverages
The title just sounds tasty. And instead of sugar, they crush up graham cracker and add that to the rim.

Lemon Vodka Punch
http://www.food.com/recipe/vodka-punch-73214
Category: Adult Beverage
This is perfect for any family gathering, especially if you know "that" uncle is going to be there. After a couple of these, you won't even notice him.

White Strawberry Lemon Sangria
http://www.kitchentreaty.com/white-strawberry-lemon-sangria/
Category: Adult Beverage
This is a fun and refreshing drink. It's easy to make and eating the fruit inside is almost as yummy as the drink. Almost!

Pink Lemonade Moscato
http://www.krystalskitsch.com/2014/12/pink-lemonade-moscato.html
Category: Adult Beverage
Two of your favorite drinks in one? Enjoy the refreshing fizz and tasty tang of this fun drink.

Cucumber Lemon Martini
https://www.youtube.com/watch?v=Q0FBENCQgxg
Category: Adult Beverages
Learn how to create this tasty beverage in under 1 minute. Yes, that fast.

Lemon Raspberry Fizz
https://www.youtube.com/watch?v=OosbVAuYeRA
Category: Adult Beverages
This festive drink is holiday perfect. Okay, it is any day perfect. You will love it no matter what time of year it is.

Other:

Lemon Garlic Salad Dressing
https://youtu.be/PjmcjXBYH2o
Category: Other
This is better than the store bought and healthier too!

Conclusion

Although lemons may not be your first choice for a tasty snack, these nutrition powerhouses can be added to your life in so many ways. When you look at lemons, they bring about thoughts of sunshine, warm days, and delicious lemonade. Even the smell of lemons can bring back wonderful memories. In fact, some studies even show that smelling lemons is enough to curb cravings.

Through this book, you've learned more about the amazing health benefits of lemons and the benefits of starting your day with warm lemon water. You've discovered how to use lemons for gorgeous skin and hair, as well as a few great cosmetic applications that can be added to your beauty regimen. You've even found out how to clean with lemons, how to use lemon oils, and how to use lemons in your favorite dishes. By now, you're a lemon expert.

Now that you're aware of all the great benefits and uses of lemons, it's important to know a few tricks for finding the perfect lemons and storing your lemons. The following are a few tips and tricks you can use with the rest of your lemon information to make the most of this beautiful, healthy citrus fruit.

Finding Quality Lemons

- Whether you plan to use your lemons for lemon water, cooking, cleaning, or your beauty routine, it's important to pick out the perfect lemons. Here are a few helpful tips to follow when choose your lemons.

- Whenever possible, choose organic lemons. This is especially important if you plan to consume the lemons or use them on your skin.

- Look for thin-skinned lemons. Thin-skinned lemons have more flesh and more juice. This means that you need to avoid lemons with thick peels. Make sure that the lemons are heavy for their size and their peels should be finely grained.

- Make sure that the lemons are fully yellow. Lemons with a green tinge have more acid in them because they're not completely ripened.

- Avoid lemons with hard patches, soft patches, dull coloring, or wrinkled peels. This means they are overripe.

Storing Your Lemons

It's important to store your lemons so they last as long as possible. Fresh lemons can be kept at room temperature, but make sure you keep them away from sunlight. At room temperature, lemons usually stay good for 7-10 days.

If you want keep lemons longer, add them to the crisper drawer in your refrigerator. You can keep lemons in the crisper drawer for as long as four weeks.

You can also store lemon zest and juice for later use. If you want to store lemon zest, dry it and store it in an airtight glass container. Make sure you keep it in a dry, cool place. You can also freeze your lemon zest. Lemon juice keeps well in the freezer. Simply squeeze lemon juice into ice cube trays. Freeze and then store the lemon cubes in freezer bags.

With these tips to guide you, you'll be able to find the best lemons available, storing them properly to maximize the life of your lemons.

References

Khaw KT, Bingham S, Welch A, et al. Relation between plasma ascorbic acid and mortality in men and women in EPIC-Norfolk prospective study: a prospective population study. European Prospective Investigation into Cancer and Nutrition. Lancet. 2001 Mar 3;357(9257):657-63. 2001.

Ogata S, Miyake Y, Yamamoto K, et al. Apoptosis induced by the flavonoid from lemon fruit (Citrus limon BURM. f.) and its metabolites in HL-60 cells. Biosci Biotechnol Biochem 2000 May;64(5):1075-8. 2000. PMID:13120

Miyake Y, Murakami A, Sugiyama Y, et al. Identification of coumarins from lemon fruit (Citrus limon) as inhibitors of in vitro tumor promotion and superoxide and nitric oxide generation. J Agric Food Chem 1999 Aug;47(8):3151-7. 1999. PMID:13130

Chemicals in Cosmetics. http://www.breastcancerfund.org/clear-science/environmental-breast-cancer-links/cosmetics/

Bloomberg Business What's On Your Face? The Ten Most Toxic Cosmetics. http://www.bloomberg.com/slideshow/2011-12-01/what-s-on-your-face-ten-most-toxic-cosmetics.html

Mercola Health. New Study Finds Major Toxins in Many Cosmetics http://articles.mercola.com/sites/articles/archive/2011/06/04/new-study-finds-major-toxins-in-many-cosmetics.aspx

Women's Health 11 Beauty Uses forLemons http://www.womenshealthmag.com/beauty/uses-for-lemons

[Click here for healthy supplements](#)

Printed in Great Britain
by Amazon